DBT Skills Workbook

A Fun Therapy Guide to Manage Stress, Anxiety, Depression, Emotions, OCD, Trauma, and Eating Disorders

(Self-Regulation for Teens)

By

Kangaroo Publications

© Copyright 2022 by (Kangaroo Publishing) - All rights reserved.

Without the prior written permission of the Publisher, no part of this publication may be stored in a retrieval system, replicated, or transferred in any form or medium, digital, scanning, recording, printing, mechanical, or otherwise, except as permitted under 1976 United States Copyright Act, section 107 or 108. Permission concerns should be directed to the publisher's permission department.

Legal Notice

This book is copyright protected. It is only to be used for personal purposes. Without the author's or publisher's permission, you cannot paraphrase, quote, copy, distribute, sell, or change any part of the information in this book.

Disclaimer Notice

This book is written and published independently. Please keep in mind that the material in this publication is solely for educational and entertaining purposes. All efforts have provided authentic, up-to-date, trustworthy, and comprehensive information. There are no express or implied assurances. The purpose of this book's material is to assist readers in having a better understanding of the subject matter. The activities, information, and exercises are provided solely for self-help information. This book is not intended to replace expert psychologists, legal, financial, or other guidance. If you require counseling, please get in touch with a qualified professional.

By reading this text, the reader accepts that the author will not be held liable for any damages, indirectly or directly, experienced due to the use of the information included herein, particularly, but not limited to, omissions, errors, or inaccuracies. As a reader, you are accountable for your decisions, actions, and consequences.

CONTENTS

INTRODUCTION..7

CHAPTER 1: DBT AND ITS EFFECTIVENESS..............10
- 1.1 DBT Fills in the Gaps..11
- 1.2 Dialectical Thinking Plays a Role in Therapy......................13
- 1.3 DBT Help with Anxiety and Stress..................................14
- 1.4 Mindfulness and Distress Tolerance Skills........................14
- 1.5 Develop Emotional Skills and Alleviate Negative Emotions......15

CHAPTER 2: DBT FOR ANXIETY AND DEPRESSION.17
- One-Mindfully..18
- Self-Soothe..19
- Radical Acceptance..21
- DEAR MAN..22
- GIVE..23
- FAST..24
- ACCEPTS..25
- IMPROVE..28
- Accepting Reality Skills..29
- Non-Judgmental Stance..32
- The Wise Mind...33
- The Function of the Emotion..33
- Paying Attention to Positives...34

CHAPTER 3: DBT FOR FEAR AND GRIEF..................36
- A Change Skill...37
- TIPP Skills..38
- Acceptance for Grief...40
- Wave Skill..41
- Dreams and Fears..42

DBT Skills for Teens and Above

Facing Fears..43

Check the Realities..44

Fear Ladder..46

Stages of Grief..47

CHAPTER 4: DBT FOR OBSESSIVE COMPULSIVE DISORDER..48

OCD Exposure Hierarchy..49

Cognitive Restructuring...50

Fear of Germs & Illness Anxiety...51

Constant Checking..52

Always Expect the Unexpected..53

Fear of Harming Others..53

Progressive Muscle Relaxation..55

Deep Breathing Exercise...56

CHAPTER 5: DBT FOR EATING DISORDER..............57

Self-Acceptance Exercises..59

Feel Your Feelings..61

Circle of Control..62

Depression and your Body...63

Set Goals...65

Use Affirmations...66

Be Gentle with Your Pain..67

CHAPTER 6: DBT FOR POST-TRAUMATIC STRESS DISORDER..70

De-Catastrophizing Worksheet..72

Challenging Unhelpful Thoughts...73

Trauma Triggers..74

Trauma Healing Worksheet..75
Regain Focus Through Physical Activity.........................76
Mindfulness Meditation..76

CHAPTER 7: IMPROVE SELF-ESTEEM THROUGH DBT..78

My View of Me...80
Improve Self-Esteem Worksheet....................................81
My Strengths..82
Self-Confidence Worksheet..83
Self-Esteem Journal..84
Mindfulness Exercises for Improving Self-Esteem........85

THE BOTTOM LINE..89

INTRODUCTION

Do you know?

Every DBT treatment is totally personalized and solely focused on the real life experiences of the individual because the core of DBT includes examining the unique background of the individual.

Many people are learning how to recognize, regulate, respond to, and prepare for circumstances that cause anxiety, thanks to DBT strategies. Finding methods to treat psychological illnesses is crucial to helping millions of people's mental health improvement.

Dialectical behavior therapy is known as DBT. This kind of cognitive behavioral therapy aims to teach people how to thrive in the present. It provides effective techniques for coping with stress, self-control, and improving one's relationships with others and oneself.

This variety of cognitive behavioral therapy tries to help patients shift from destructive thought patterns to constructive behavioral adjustments. It empowers individuals to control unpleasant, demanding, or "anxious" emotions. DBT was initially created for people with borderline personality disorder (BPD). Since its inception, mental health professionals have used it to treat patients with depression, eating disorders, PTSD, drug dependence, and anxiety, as well as other mental health-related problems.

One-on-one treatment sessions are the main component of this therapy. A therapist guides the client as they learn effective DBT treatments for anxiety. The client then employs DBT approaches for anxiety to improve emotion control and management.

You could believe that dialectical behavior therapy (DBT) and cognitive behavioral therapy (CBT) generally have a lot in common. Of course, there are similarities because DBT is a subtype of CBT. But DBT also has unique characteristics that set it apart from most CBT strategies.

Similar to CBT, DBT focuses on assisting individuals in addressing their dysfunctional thinking and behavior by altering their thought patterns. CBT is typically only used for a brief time and is frequently used to achieve one or two specified aims.

DBT, on the other hand, concentrates on the psychosocial facets of daily life. Although many people struggle with their thought and behavior habits, but interpersonal connections are frequently where these problems are most upsetting. The emphasis on interpersonal relationships in DBT explains why group therapy includes a DBT-specific component. Clients are given a chance to practice relational skills in a secure and encouraging environment by incorporating group dynamics into the learning environment, which has proven successful.

Using the clients' past is another way DBT varies from conventional CBT. Both acknowledge the past while working toward a better present, but unlike CBT, where this conversation is frequently the main focus of therapy, DBT does not. DBT holds that while one can learn from their experience, problems are always founded on current ideas and behaviors, and it is in the present that these issues will be resolved.

By keeping in mind the benefits of DBT therapy for different mental illnesses, this book is written in an easy and understandable manner to guide readers throughout their recovery journey. Multiple exercises and activities will help you to overcome your emotions and feelings. Mindfulness and Meditation techniques are a source of relaxation and for keeping you calm till the end. So, keep on reading and explore the way to get out of your mental issues.

CHAPTER 1

DBT AND ITS EFFECTIVENESS

DBT is an empirically supported therapy that balances acceptance and change. It enables the development of abilities in interpersonal interaction, attentive awareness, the capacity to tolerate discomfort, and emotion regulation.

In DBT, there are four modules:

Learning techniques to practice being fully conscious and present at the moment is the foundation of mindfulness. *Mindfulness* is a technique that has its roots in Buddhist philosophy and strongly emphasizes the present moment.

Managing conflict and communicating assertively yet being empathetic toward others are examples of *interpersonal effectiveness*. Skills acquired could be ways to say no, deal with interpersonal conflict, and ask for what you need.

Distress Tolerance is the capacity to accept, make sense of, and endure suffering. Learning to experience strong feelings like rage without reacting rashly or employing unhealthy coping mechanisms to lessen distress, for self-soothing, staying in the present moment, and using acceptance skills are some techniques for coping with stress.

Emotion regulation is the process of identifying, naming, and modifying emotions. Assistance in developing emotional self-control and altering how you respond to situations. The following skills can be used: recognizing and naming emotions, identifying barriers to changing feelings, enhancing positive emotional experiences, raising mindfulness of current emotions, doing the opposite action, and using techniques for distress tolerance.

DBT teaches you how to handle challenging circumstances that come up in daily life. Therapy exercises aim to increase your motivation and support you in using new abilities to address certain problems in your life. DBT has benefited many who struggle with depression, substance addiction, anger control, PTSD, and disordered eating. Still, it can also be helpful to anybody who wants to learn how to control their emotions and cope with challenging situations.

1.1 DBT Fills in the Gaps

Using dialectical behavior therapy, certain behaviors can be changed from the inside out. For example; DBT gets to the root of an individual's addiction problems. A person can identify the causes of their addiction and make the required changes that impact all facets of their life when they reflect on and relive past experiences with their counselor.

DBT therapies are all unique. Every DBT treatment is tailored and solely focused on the real-life experiences of the patient because the core of DBT entails examining the individual's unique background.

The field of DBT is still expanding. Dialectical Behavior Therapy is now only offered by a few drug recovery clinics, but this number is rising. DBT is used by patients in addiction treatment clinics with great success rates, and knowledge of this is quickly spreading.

Buddhist teachings provide the basis of dialectical behavior therapy. The core of DBT is Zen Buddhist training to develop self-awareness. This increased awareness is used by DBT counselors to assist the client in understanding how their behaviors influence others and vice versa.

DBT emphasizes enhancing one's perception of oneself. When a person needs their self-image to be restored, DBT can help. DBT aids in boosting a person's confidence in even the most trying circumstances by helping them learn more effective ways to communicate with others.

People with cutting problems (self-harm) benefit from dialectical behavior therapy. DBT assists people who struggle with cutting and other forms of self-harm in better understanding their triggers and altering the thought processes that result in self-harm.

DBT aids in the development of assertiveness. In DBT, there is a significant amount of "role-playing." Many of these scenarios teach the person to say "NO" to the temptations and unfavorable influences that have dragged them deeper into the addiction cycle.

DBT promotes acceptance. Training the person to be tolerant of others, especially in circumstances where their perspectives are different or may be seen as a possible danger, is another distinguishing feature of DBT.

DBT was created to aid those with borderline personality disorder. The early applications of DBT were in treating borderline personality disorder (BPD), where patients benefited from the therapy's restored assertiveness and confidence.

DBT offers more than just a temporary solution to the issue. The fact that dialectical behavior therapy is not a Band-Aid or short-term solution for drug addiction, alcoholism, or mental diseases may be the most crucial thing to understand about it. Instead, DBT addresses the underlying reasons for the behavior and equips individuals with the skills they need to succeed in any circumstance.

1.2 Dialectical Thinking Plays a Role in Therapy

Dr. Marsha Linehan, a psychologist, created dialectical behavior therapy while working with women hospitalized after making major attempts at suicide or self-harm. Dr. Linehan, a medical expert passionate about providing her patients with successful treatments, began by using Cognitive Behavioral Therapy (CBT), a form of therapy that encourages altering thoughts, feelings, and actions to control and lessen anxiety.

The gold standard for treating anxiety is often CBT. But Dr. Linehan discovered that conventional CBT wasn't effective with her clients. She felt that CBT's focus on altering thoughts and actions did not go far enough in helping her clients accept their current situation. People often found ideas like cognitive distortions to suggest that their feelings and thoughts were incorrect, which made the CBT approaches alone invalidating to them. Dr. Linehan saw that a new approach was required to respect and support the reality that underlay clients' experiences.

This is where dialectical behavior therapy (DBT) comes in. It is a subset of cognitive behavioral therapy that strongly focuses on mindfulness and dialectical thought. DBT emphasizes acceptance of events as they are in this presentation as an equally crucial component to treating symptoms as issues to be solved. It is one of many therapies that use acceptance-based behavior (ABBT).

The core of DBT is dialectical thinking, a philosophical position that holds that two seemingly conflicting ideas or truths can coexist. For instance, a person seeking treatment can require motivation to change and acceptance of where they are. In other words, they must acknowledge that everything is just as it should be while also realizing that they must improve and work harder to bring about a change for the better.

1.3 DBT Help with Anxiety and Stress

In our lives, emotions play crucial roles. Fear can push us to act and defend ourselves when there is a danger to our life, or wellbeing; therefore, primary emotions associated with anxiety, such as terror, can occasionally make perfect sense. However, there are instances when negative or unproductive emotions, such as dread, surface. Anxiety and distress can result from an inability to control and cope with these emotions.

DBT involves learning cognitive and emotional skills (acquisition) and then using those abilities in your daily life (generalization). DBT generally addresses challenging and distressing emotions and can help you strengthen your capacity for regulating or managing the emotions you feel when you experience them and how you express your feelings.

1.4 Mindfulness and Distress Tolerance Skills

The DBT skills training group teaches clients strategies like mindfulness and distress tolerance that help them accept the present moment willingly rather than resisting it. These methods can include deep breathing, numbering to ten, or holding an ice cube to bring consciousness and acceptance to the present. Such activities help us decide to accept what is occurring right now.

Observing and describing feelings and having a methodical toolset for changing emotions you wish to change are among the emotion regulation skills taught in DBT. These strategies involve verifying the facts of a situation, resisting the temptation to act on emotion, and problem-solving to alter the circumstances that led to an emotional response.

The main objective of DBT is to change and influence emotions but to get to this stage; it is crucial to comprehend and grasp where these emotions originate from and why they develop. One of the key aspects of DBT that sets it apart from conventional CBT is the "understanding and acknowledging" stage, which encourages the focused and non-judgmental description and observation of emotional events. This component benefits DBT for various mental health issues, including anxiety disorders. This is due to the skills you acquire to allow you to distinguish between emotions and facts and successfully work with and manage emotions.

1.5 Develop Emotional Skills and Alleviate Negative Emotions

Individual therapy with a qualified therapist, group skill training, skills coaching (typically available by phone), and the psychiatrist's participation in a consultation team are all components of comprehensive DBT. All of these elements work together to ensure that DBT provides skills you may use to feel more in charge of how you think and interact with the world around you. If you have an anxiety problem, you undoubtedly already know how vital and empowering it is to feel in charge of your life.

For example; emotional management techniques like Opposite Action helped Brenda confront her fears rather than run away from them. She was able to embrace the moment thanks to mindfulness techniques, and she was able to enrich her life with greater happiness and purpose through fulfilling relationships. Healthy life skills that we can all incorporate into our daily lives are offered and taught by DBT. These skills will stick with us for years.

CHAPTER 2

DBT FOR ANXIETY AND DEPRESSION

Though dialectical behavior therapy (DBT) is mostly used to treat borderline personality disorder (BPD), its core principles are quite straightforward. The dialectic theory is used to promote both acceptance and transformation at the same time. This enables those suffering to embrace the present while realizing that change is inevitable for the future.

DBT is an empirically supported treatment, which is supported by research. It is divided into two main parts: individual therapy and skill development.

Skills provide specific answers to very common situations. It addresses widespread problems even though it was intended for people with BPD. This implies that anyone can truly utilize it. These following DBT techniques and activities can aid people in managing their anxiety.

One-Mindfully

A skill called One-Mindfully argues that being present in the moment can be a trickily restorative activity. People frequently spend their present-day lives daydreaming about the past or the future. As we become fixated on what we've previously done incorrectly or are guaranteed to do incorrectly, this can easily cause anxiety.

This goal is to better equip us to deal with future issues.

Planning and practice are undoubtedly essential. But persistent anxiety can be debilitating. It can cause psychological harm because it is harder to recognize and take action on effective decisions.

The truth is that when we completely engage in the now, we are better equipped to handle obstacles as they emerge in the future. In societies, professions, and nations where the motto is "work 'til you keel over," this idea may seem alien. Self-care and upkeep are sometimes disregarded yet crucial aspects of productivity.

Encouraging less dwelling on the past and enabling us to approach challenges in the future from a more mentally stable position also helps combat anxiety. It aids in avoiding overextension, which is a precursor to burnout.

Self-Soothe

In DBT, the idea of self-soothing relates to our capacity to reduce emotional turbulence by establishing a sense of physical reality and concentrating on physical cues. The five senses—taste, smell, vision, hearing, and touch—can all be used for this.

This implies that there are countless possible applications for this skill, depending on what the individual finds to be most useful. It can aid anxiety sufferers in "getting out of" their heads to regain a sense of reality. One could, for instance, suck on hard candy and evaluate the taste and sensation. They can also find refuge in a favorite song or an animal's cuddly, calming touch.

For those who experience anxiety, the activity can be especially beneficial because it temporarily replaces ruminating and worrying. The ability to think more objectively and calmly can then be used after taking a break from meditating. This should either give the person a brief break from their anxiety or enable them to devise more effective solutions to whatever is causing it.

Fortunately, this skills aids in dealing with both the anticipation of worry and the effects of an emotionally upsetting occurrence. For self-soothing worksheet, go to the next page and try the technique.

Self-Soothing Skill Worksheet

Write 5 things you SEE right now

1. _____
2. _____
3. _____
4. _____
5. _____

Write 4 things you FEEL right now

1. _____
2. _____
3. _____
4. _____

Write 3 things you HEAR right now

1. _____
2. _____
3. _____

Write 2 things you SMELL right now

1. _____
2. _____

Write 1 thing you can TASTE right now

1. _____

Write out some positive thoughts

1. _____
2. _____
3. _____
4. _____

DBT Skills for Teens and Above

Radical Acceptance

Radical acceptance is one of the harder DBT skills to learn and may take more work. It entails embracing the world as it is at that precise time.

Sounds very simple, doesn't it?

But what if you accept a loved one's death, the end of a relationship, a humiliating mistake at work, or a catastrophic error?

Radical acceptance aims to acknowledge that these unpleasant feelings are genuine and authentic rather than running from them. Therefore, one should attempt to change the experience or find peace with it.

Anxiety sufferers, who often wonder why and how something happened instead of considering how they will accept or escape the situation, can have a profoundly negative impact on their lives. The belief that a deeper comprehension of the issue will change it underlies a lot of anxiety. This is frequently just slightly false.

This is because ruminating is a preventative deterrent to being unprepared for a problem or situation. However, it can be used in pathologically harmful ways. This can result in people exerting enormous effort while realizing their circumstances never seem to improve.

DEAR MAN

The goal in learning the DEARMAN skill is to improve our ability to communicate with others effectively, which will enable us to meet our requirements and forge lasting relationships.

What is the current circumstance?(if necessary)

Keep it factual. Clearly state your reaction to the person. Share your thoughts and feelings regarding the circumstance. Never presume that the other person understands your feelings.

Make a statement obvious when you say "no" or ask for what you want. Never presume that other people will understand what you desire. Keep in mind that nobody can read your thinking.

Explain the advantages of receiving what you want or need in advance to reinforce (or reward) the other person. If necessary, make clear the drawbacks of not getting what you want or need.

Be mindful, maintain your goals in mind. Hold onto your position. Avoid being sidetracked. Don't stray from the subject. Talk in a "Broken record" fashion. Ask for what you want repeatedly. Or simply reply "No" and keep voicing your viewpoint. Repeating the same action over and over will suffice. Ignore any assaults. Ignore any verbal abuse, threats, or attempts to shift the conversation elsewhere if the other person does so. Never answer an assault back. Avoid being distracted. Just continue to make your case.

Make a strong, successful, and capable impression. Make eye contact, speak with confidence, and move with assurance. No stuttering, muttering, glancing at the ground, or backing away.

When negotiating, be prepared to part with something. Offer and solicit other approaches to the issue. Cut back on your request. Say "no," but then offer to take another action or find a different solution to the issue. Consider what will be effective.

GIVE

It serves as a reminder to be sincere, keep an interest in what we're doing, validates our actions, and be approachable. Reviewing each of these in further detail can help.

Be Sincere.

You can act honestly and be your actual self by being genuine. Sometimes when we try to fit in, we compromise our beliefs and create internal conflict.

Keep Your Interest.

We enable and demand reciprocity in the relationship by expressing interest in someone. This enables both of you to understand that the connection is a two-way street and ensures that you can contribute to it. Body language can also be used to convey interest. Do you still make eye contact? Do you have your hands on something, or are you slouching and staring at your phone?

To Verify.

In a relationship, to validate is to accept what you have heard without passing judgment or attempting to change the other person. Instead of pressing your plan, you focus on the other person and listen to their needs. Although it can be challenging, there are times when we just want to be heard. Have you ever experienced that before?

Have A Calm Attitude.

Last but not least, keeping things informal promotes a successful relationship. Use of humor (where appropriate), a smile, and an easygoing attitude are all examples of calm manners. Relationships can only take rigidity so far.

FAST

The FAST skill is a crucial part of communication because it enables you to uphold your self-respect, forces you to be honest about the issues at hand (even if you are discreet in how you express them), and prevents you from compromising your morals or integrity.

Be Fair

Be fair to both the other person and yourself. Always remember to respect the sentiments and desires of the other person and your own.

Don't Apologize Too Much

No excuses for being alive or for asking anything. There are no excuses for disagreeing or having a viewpoint. No lowering your head or projecting an embarrassed expression.

Maintain Your Principles

Don't compromise your morals or integrity for unimportant reasons. Stick to your guns and be clear about what you feel is a moral or valuable way of thinking and acting.

Be Honest

Avoid lying. If you are not helpless, don't act like it. Don't lie or invent justifications.

ACCEPTS

Distress tolerance techniques are meant to divert us and help us go through challenging emotional situations slowly. The abbreviation ACCEPTS is a helpful method to remember this ability.

Activities

Pay close attention to a job you have to finish. Think of TV and movie rentals. Organize a space in your home. Find a gathering to attend. Engage in online gaming. Exercise.

Contributions

Do some volunteer work. Assist a friend or member of your family. Bring a smile to someone's face. Donate items you no longer require.

Comparisons

Compare your current state of well-being to a previous one. Consider those who are coping similarly to you or less successfully than you.

Emotions

Read heartfelt novels, short stories, or old letters. Visit emotive movies and watch emotional television. Play some affecting music.

Pushing Away

Leave the situation alone for a bit to push it away. Leave the situation in your mind. Put a barrier between you and the circumstance in your mind. Remove ideas and visuals from your mind.

Thoughts

Count anything up to ten, such as the colors in a painting, a poster, or the sky. In your head, recite the lyrics to a song. Solve puzzles or observe TV and read.

Sensations

Strenuously squeeze a rubber ball. Tune in to loud music. Go outside in the snow or rain. Shower either hot or cold.

These are some ACCEPTS activities. Try these during a certain event of your mental issue and complete the worksheet on the next page.

Accepts
Effectiveness Worksheet

Prompting Event:
_____
_____

The ACCEPTS skill I tried was:
_____

I chose this skill because:
_____
_____

The way I used this skill was to:
_____
_____
_____

Due to this skill I was able to avoid the following reaction:
_____
_____
_____

This skill was successful or unsuccessful because:
_____
_____
_____

IMPROVE

The goal of the IMPROVE skill is to improve the current situation by switching out the immediate trigger for negative feelings for a more uplifting action, making the situation more pleasant and tolerable.

Imagery: Use imagery to make the moment better. Think of a breathtaking location in the mountains or on the beach. Think of a secure area in your house.

Meaning: Add meaning to the present. Find significance or purpose in the things you do every day.

Prayer: Use prayer to make this moment better. Ask your superior being for strength.

Relaxation: Use relaxation to make the present better. Take a hot bath, massage your neck, and exhale slowly.

One: Enhance the present by doing one thing at once. Pay close attention to this instant.

Vacation: From adulthood, improve the moment with a vacation. Take a walk in the woods or on the beach.

Encouragement: Make the current situation better by encouraging yourself. Say encouraging things out loud to yourself.

Accepting Reality Skills

This is a crucial skill that helps people who struggle with emotional deregulation and the typical person.

Fighting the suffering and pain that are a natural part of being a human is a problem that affects many people in our society. Dealing with reality is a good remedy for this. DBT and Acceptance and Commitment Therapy (ACT) emphasize that thriving requires accepting our reality, including its unpleasant features.

Since there are many crafty ways we come up with to ignore the truth of our circumstances, it can be more difficult to practice and develop this talent than it first appears to be.

These examples can help clarify when we tend to resist reality and how to stop this behavior:

You have to get home quickly, stopping at every red light. You take a big breath and tell yourself, "This is what it is," choosing not to get upset. "When it turns green, I'll go home."

Your car needs fuel, but gas prices have climbed. You take a deep breath and tell yourself "there is nothing you can do to change the situation. I want gas. Getting furious won't solve the problem".

Your automobile is in the shop, so you must walk to work. Even though it's close, it's pouring. You exhale deeply and declare, "It's only rain. When I get to work, I'll dry off using a towel I bring".

There are some suggestions for developing this ability at the moment that is both amazing and practical:

- Recognize how you are battling the truth of your circumstance. Recognize that your reaction is a result of a situation you cannot control;

- Despite how challenging or painful it may be, keep reminding yourself of reality;
- Think about the causes of the current reality, and utilize the talent of non-judgment to remember that this is a random event that was caused by a million other things that are out of your control.
- Accept it with all your beings, mind, soul, and spirit. Pay attention to both the physical (such as posture and the "fight-or-flight" response) and spiritual (you may "understand" that this is true, but you don't "feel" like it is real) indicators of resistance to reality.

While by no means thorough or necessary to accept reality, these actions can be useful in the short term. Use the worksheet on the next page to practice reality acceptance.

Reality Acceptance Worksheet

Realities that I am refusing to accept:

1._____
2._____
3._____
4._____
5._____

Behaviors that I do when I am refusing to accept a reality (may look like a tantrum, giving up, manipulating, arguing, etc).

1._____
2._____
3._____
4._____
5._____

How I experience SUFFERING when I refuse to accept reality:

1._____
2._____
3._____
4._____
5._____

Non-Judgmental Stance

Being objective is a skill that requires effort, but the benefits can be enormous. When you are non-judgmental, you refrain from giving things a numerical worth. Learning non-judgment allows us to stand back from a challenging circumstance and recognize that the value judgments we form are based on facts (the realities of what is occurring) and the sentiments we are feeling in response.

For instance, you might be in backed-up traffic from an accident and think, "People are such morons." This could be translated as "I'm trapped at a standstill in traffic because there's an accident up ahead" if you try not to be judgmental. "I'm angry about this."

When you separate a judgment into a fact and an emotional response, you not only lessen the emotion(s) you are feeling but also give yourself more capacity to consider solutions and make wise choices.

Let's say you are currently considering how greedy your important other (partner) is acting. Using non-judgment may help you articulate the problem ("My spouse is not assisting me with this issue, and that gets me upset and disappointed") and identify a solution ("This is not a good use of my energy and time. "), as opposed to just saying "My partner is so selfish." ("I'll talk to my spouse about how I feel and try and negotiate a resolution with them about how their refusal to assist me with this situation makes me feel.").

When you deal with difficult emotional situations in a way that makes you feel proud of yourself, it can help you control your emotions and come up with clever solutions to issues and boost your self-esteem and respect.

The Wise Mind

The "smart mind" is defined in this section as the point where the emotional and rational minds converge. It is characterized by the capacity to acknowledge and appreciate your sentiments while still reacting to them logically. It is a harmony between the two minds. Understanding your inner wise mind is important skill in DBT.

The Function of the Emotion

You can use the Function of Emotion Regulation to determine the purpose of an emotional response you've experienced in the past.

The questions and steps on the worksheet are as follows:

- What happened to cause this?
- What did you make of it?
- What was the strength of the feeling (0–100)?

To determine the purpose(s) of the feeling, use the following:

- Has the emotion affected others' conduct or communicated something to them? If so, explain;
- Did the feeling prompt you to act or organize yourself? If so, explain.
- Did the emotion inform you, affect how you perceived things, or cause you to conclude? If so, elaborate.

These inquiries help the person comprehend the relationship between a catalyzing event and the emotional response to the experience and how the emotional reaction affects both the self and others.

Paying Attention to Positives

Increasing good emotions can be a useful strategy for overcoming challenging emotions. Focus on your pleasant daily experiences (short-term experiences) and the larger, more significant ones to develop this skill (long-term experiences). Try mindfulness to relish great events while concentrating on establishing and maintaining positive relationships.

Letting go of the unpleasant also affects emotion regulation, which is the opposite of savoring the positive. Acknowledge that obsessing over unpleasant feelings all the time is unhealthy for your wellbeing. Practice watching, describing, and accepting your feelings without letting them control you. To work on your positive thoughts, use the worksheet below.

Paying Attention to Positive

Identify and write some of your negative thoughts and then think about how you can change these into positive thoughts.

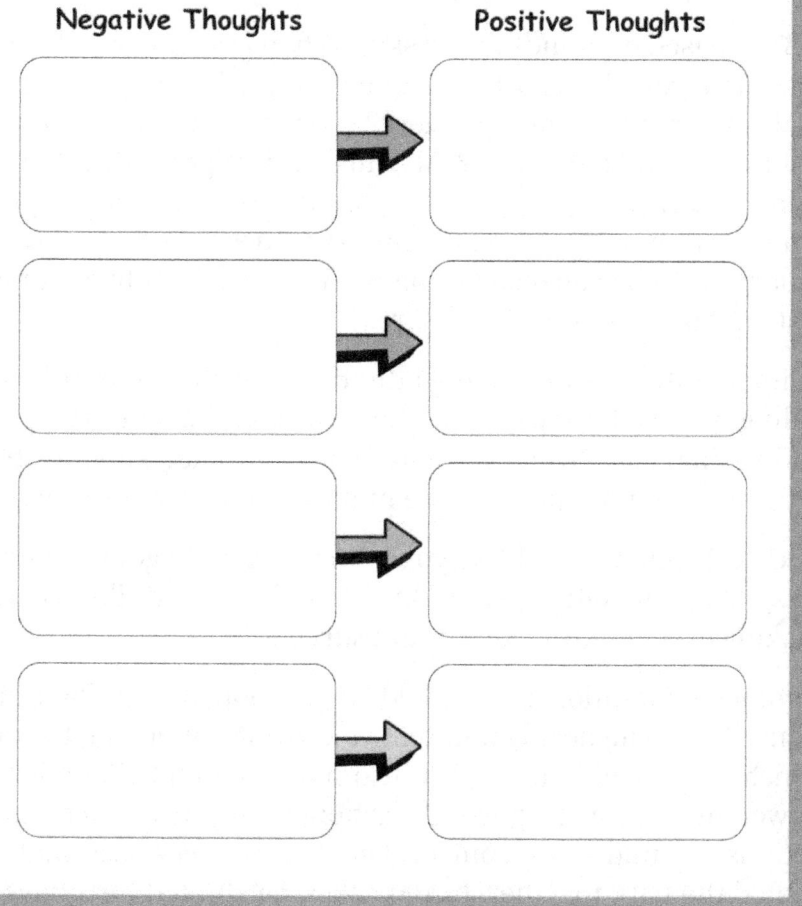

DBT Skills for Teens and Above

CHAPTER 3

DBT FOR FEAR AND GRIEF

DBT is based on mindfulness skill. When grieving, we frequently ask ourselves, "What I have done wrong?" "Why did I conclude that my child needed surgery?" What if I weren't on that roadway at that moment? My husband might still be around. Additionally, we speculate about an unrealized future, trying to figure out how to recreate our identities after what we had thought it to be collapsed in on us. We are left feeling damaged, lost, and unable to see the future.

Being mindful means paying attention to the present. It involves telling yourself to pay attention to that instant. It involves addressing any "what if" and "could, would, should" before returning your attention to the moment and what is occurring.

The next time you feel like you won't be able to get through this loss, tell yourself: "Yes, it hurts so bad. And I'm currently making every effort to get by and survive."

Another illustration is, "I could have stopped him from killing himself." Inhale deeply and tell, "I know it's an avoidable death, which is incredibly painful. I also have to admit that I have no power over another person's actions. Only my reactions and actions are under my control. Our family was affectionate. We visited the park together, baked cakes, celebrated birthdays, and built bonfires. Instead of focusing on the 4% of parenting I did poorly, I should concentrate on the 96% I did correctly."

Furthermore, it can take some time. You might wonder about "what if" and "could would should." Be calm with yourself since it will take time.

A Change Skill

This skill emphasizes achieving your goals while fostering connections and preserving self-respect. Here is an example of how this might be used in a situation of loss where well-meaning family members attempt to drag you back into the open before you are prepared.

__Example:__

Consider the following scenario: Even though it has been three years since your child's passing, your sister has complained to other family members about how you always bring up her passing. She feels uncomfortable as a result, which has angered and saddened you. She's also voiced concern that you continue to visit your child's cemetery because, in her opinion, it shows you aren't "moving on" from the loss the way you need to.

Here are some ways you can use DBT techniques and "I feel" expressions to deal with this because it's upsetting. You want to tell your sister in a considerate and respectful manner that keeps your relationship intact while allowing you to be heard rather than feeling angry and frustrated. This can be written in a letter as well.

Defining the Situation: "Every time I mention my dear Denise's passing, you interrupt me and shift the subject. Furthermore, you've indicated that you don't like it when I go to my child's grave, even though she passed away many years ago.

TIPP Skills

TIPP stands for temperature, intensive exercise, purposeful breathing, and paired muscle relaxation. TIPP skills are essential skills that you can employ to transition out of crisis mode and into a stable condition. While they won't remove the cause of the pain, they do provide good coping mechanisms for when there is severe pain.

Temperature

Our bodies warm up when we are depressed or angry. You can run or stroll outside in the cold or hold an ice cube to counteract that effect. Changing your body's temperature aids in both a physical and an emotional brain reset. Dipping your face in freezing water for 30 seconds is a suicide prevention technique.

Intense Exercise

Match your level of exercise intensity to your current state of mind. It's not necessary to hold a world record in the running. Until you're exhausted, move quickly, run to the end of the street, jump rope, run the stairs, or engage in any other activity that, in your opinion, is intense. Spending that energy on vigorous activity improves your oxygen flow and reduces stress, and it's impossible to remain dangerously agitated while you're fatigued. You can express your strong feelings through it.

Paced Breathing

Breathing significantly impacts easing emotional pain. Breathing techniques help to relieve worry or manage bereavement.

Paired Muscle Relaxation

I refer to this as rigid to ragdoll. A muscle is tightened repeatedly before being relaxed and given time to rest. Your breathing and pulse rate slow as your muscles become more relaxed and demand less oxygen. Try this method by concentrating on specific muscles, like those in your arms and back. For five seconds, tense the muscles as much as you can. Then release.

Acceptance for Grief

The phrase "radical acceptance for grief" means same what it tells. It is a method for fully investing and participating in accepting the truth, no matter how hard it may be. Loss-related emotions can make you feel like they'll harm you, but they won't.

While grieving, acceptance encourages us to reach the heart of our melancholy without passing judgment on ourselves or making excuses.

Have you made any efforts to put your suffering off? Knowing that these are the cornerstones of emotional healing, what you can do to alleviate your pain?

Even while it seems awful and impossible to survive during acute pain moments, which last 60 to 90 seconds, no feeling is ever truly permanent. And because millions, if not billions, of people, have survived before you, you will also. So, if you let your feelings come up, you may stay with them until they pass, and after the discomfort is gone, you can divert your attention to something else.

Pushing them aside will slow down your healing process and keep you in the process of suffering much longer than necessary.

Wave Skill

Letting your emotions be there without acting abruptly is what it means to "ride the wave." In other words, when we are overly emotional, we can make extremely bad mistakes that we will regret afterwards. This skill teaches you to ride your emotions' waves rather than fight them as a surfer does. Emotional tsunamis are common during difficult times. It can get worse if you try to deal with your strong feelings in a dangerous or unproductive way. This ability is all about enduring difficult situations without resorting to unhealthy overcompensation.

To ride the wave entails accepting the experience and managing it without altering it. It may feel odd to ride the wave and stay with the discomfort because the urge is more often to want to escape from and remedy an uncomfortable condition of being. But no feeling lasts forever. The worst of them lasts between 60 and 90 seconds, and they are constantly changing.

Accepting unpleasant feelings can alleviate your suffering, even though doing so can cause extreme fear and appear illogical. Would you like to extend it?

For instance, you could believe that downing a bottle of alcohol will help you cope with your grief, but in reality, it will worsen the matters. Because your decision making is already bad while you're grieving and considerably get worse when you've drink too much, you might get in the car and drive, endangering others. You might even develop a dependence or addiction.

Dreams and Fears

It is a dreams and fears tree. Think of your dreams and fears and write down on petals.

Dreams and Fears Tree

DBT Skills for Teens and Above

Facing Fears

My Fears

- Big Fear
- Medium Fear
- Small Fear

What is the Fear?

How does it make you feel?

Check the Realities

We make a lot of assumptions. Therefore, it is beneficial to review the information, especially if we feel irrational or emotional.

Taking the lost child's example further, I was certain that no one in my friends would call me after the memorial service because my child just died and was labeled as "no enjoy at all, ever." Until I confronted my absurd "oh poor me" delusions by considering the realities, I had imagined all kinds of situations in which they, my pals, were ignoring me. I inquired myself if I truly believed they were not phoning because they were avoiding or suddenly disliking me.

When I gave it some thinking, I understood how absurd that notion was. What emotions would I have if a friend of mine lost a kid to self-harm? Perhaps they are unsure of what I intended to say. Could they have been afraid to see my tragedy? They had families and busy lives and probably weren't even understanding my daily suffering, let alone know what could be done. Did they even know I wanted to go outside and have to hear back from them? How could I make my intentions clear to them?

Smoke signals would not be effective. Brooding and remaining silent wasn't going to help. I wouldn't accomplish anything by sitting about and blaming everything for my problems. As a result, I thought to invite everyone to a party. It was an indication that I didn't want to separate myself and that I needed their companionship.

They all arrived, brought the drinks and food because I couldn't do it myself, and I just gave the space. We enjoyed spending the evening on my balcony. Yes, some will never communicate. Their loss! However, most people want to act but what to do because every one of us has various desires, and they cannot read our minds. Therefore, we must tell at least one member of the friend circle about that.

Fear Ladder

Fear Ladder

Start by writing down the fear that you are facing. Then for each step of the ladder, write down one thing you can do to face that fear head-on. Make sure to reward yourself for each step you take.

The fear I am facing is_____

DBT Skills for Teens and Above

46

Stages of Grief

My Stages of Grief

Instruction: Describe how each of the stages of grief has affected you.

Denial: "This can't be happening"
___

Anger: "Why is this happening to me?"
___

Bargaining: "I will do anything to change this."
___

Depression: "What's the point of going on after this loss?"
___

Acceptance: "I know what happened, and I can't change it. Now I need to cope."
___

CHAPTER 4

DBT FOR OBSESSIVE COMPULSIVE DISORDER

Obsessive behavior frequently has a superstitious component, with the afflicted believing that their constant checking, counting, or cleaning would "avoid something horrible happening." Frequently, it's utterly unclear what exactly that "something" could be.

OCD can be defined as a severe dread of not performing a task (whether it be a physical task like cleaning or a mental task like counting or checking). The worry of resisting it drives the compulsion.

OCD frequently varies in severity, from terribly awful to quite bad to scarcely perceptible. Get a general understanding of how individual manages stress in their lives and what isn't satisfying, so you can help yourself. This is important because it tends to get worse when background stress levels are high.

In treating obsessive-compulsive disorder (OCD), cognitive restructuring and exposure and response prevention are two key components of Dialectic-behavioral treatment (DBT). Most OCD patients who get DBT treatment begin observing improvements within a few weeks.

OCD treatment is typically brief but has therapeutic advantages that last. Depending on how severe someone's OCD symptoms are, DBT typically entails weekly, one-hour therapy sessions lasting six months or less. To benefit the most from DBT for most disorders, the individual must put in effort outside therapy sessions.

OCD Exposure Hierarchy

Exposure Hierarchy

Create a list of anxiety-producing situations, beginning with the most distressing and ending with the least distressing. Rank how distressing each item is on a scale of 1 to 10.

	Anxiety, Obsession, or Compulsion Trigger	Distress Level (1 - 10)
1		
2		
3		
4		
5		
6		
7		
8		
9		
10		

DBT Skills for Teens and Above

Cognitive Restructuring

Cognitive Restructuring

Use this worksheet to begin challenging irrational thoughts to move towards a better understanding of yourself and the world around you.

_____

What is the Evidence for/against this thought?

Am I basing the thought on fact or feeling?

Is this thought black and white or more complicated?

Could I be misinterpreting the evidence or making assumptions?

How would other people interpret the situation?

Fear of Germs & Illness Anxiety

Angie, a 46-year-old residence mother, is constantly concerned about getting sick and being unable to look after her kids. She is so afraid that she goes to great lengths to protect herself from germs. While her kids are at school, she cleans her house for hours daily. She feels driven to wash her hands or take a shower as soon as she touches anything she thinks is unclean. She washes her hands so often that her hands and arms are exceedingly dry, red, chapped, and cracked.

The DBT will delve into Angie's early experiences with illness, hygiene, and the availability and well-being. Discussing Angie's perceived benefits of these intrusive thoughts and what she receives from them will establish when these obsessive thoughts started and what was going on then.

Then, the worksheets will determine Angie's intrusive thoughts using exposure to a utilized object or tool. They will seek to refute these beliefs, demonstrating the harm caused by her actions through specific justifications. Angie will use the new thought patterns to direct her behavior going forward as she works to grasp these true repercussions vs. the seeming benefits of her compulsions.

Constant Checking

Tony has just started college, moved into his first home independently, and has OCD-checking tendencies. He makes sure the stove is off before he departs from his residence. He then goes to the restroom to ensure the sink's faucet is not running. He turns on and off the water, ensuring the handle is fully in the off position. He repeats it eight times. He then goes back to ensure the burner is off before leaving again. He locks his front door after leaving his house. He is quickly concerned that the stove is on, so he returns twice more to ensure. He secures his front door by locking it and turning the handle eight times to ensure it is locked and won't open.

The therapy will look into Tony's early experiences with certainty and absolutes, as well as his exposure to traumatic events and any guilt that Tony may have received as a kid. The worksheets and activities will continue to talk about the validity of Tony's memory and level of confidence, as well as the chance of equipment being turned on after being confirmed to be off.

To assist Tony in recognizing intrusive thoughts, the therapy will role-play Tony's daily routine of leaving his apartment and urge him not to recheck anything. In order to rewire Tony's thoughts so he can challenge them when they come, the DBT will examine with him why he questions himself. To move on without preoccupation, Tony will discuss what is discovered while addressing the underlying issues connected to these obsessive thoughts and coping mechanisms.

Always Expect the Unexpected

Any moment or any place can be the source of compulsive thinking. When old or even new ones appear, don't be shocked. Don't be surprised by it. Be ready to use your therapeutic tools wherever and whenever you need to. Also, let your family know immediately if any new thoughts come to mind so they can stay updated.

Fear of Harming Others

Sam is a high school freshman. She worries that they will suffer a major injury if she touches someone first. She stays away from physical contact and social interactions as a result of this phobia. She thinks that the only way to keep herself from getting wounded if she unintentionally touches someone is to become hurt herself. Every time she fails to avoid touch, she uses a razor blade that she keeps with her and creates tiny cuts on her arms and legs.

The therapist will investigate the origin of these concerns when they first appeared and any childhood events that might have contributed to them. To determine if there has been any trauma in her past, they will also talk about when this began and a record of her physical contacts.

Sam's therapy will talk about Sam's current perceptions of self-harm's advantages and the risk that someone might get hurt accidentally. The DBT will role-play Sam during recovery to discover intrusive thoughts and maybe any underlying sadness, anxiety, post-traumatic stress disorder (PTSD), or other mental health issues that may be contributing factors. Her home environment will also be evaluated. Sam will work to question these habits and continue to keep a journal of her thoughts, which she will bring to therapy to work through. She will keep track of when these thoughts start, where she is, and what she does in response.

Progressive Muscle Relaxation

It is a simple and easy exercise to do at home when you start having OCD thoughts.

Progressive Muscle Relaxation

	Take 3 Deep Breaths
	Squeeze your foot for 5 seconds. Relax
	Squeeze your leg for 5 seconds. Relax
	Squeeze your stomach for 5 seconds. Relax
	Shrug your shoulders for 5 seconds. Relax
	Squeeze your arm & hand for 5 seconds. Relax
	Squeeze your whole body for 5 seconds. Relax
	Take 3 Deep Breaths

DBT Skills for Teens and Above

Deep Breathing Exercise

After trying breathing exercises, make an evaluation list for yourself.

Deep Breathing Reflection

1. How do you feel after trying out these new breathing exercises?

2. Which is your favourite deep breathing exercise?

3. Why do you think deep breathing exercises are important?

CHAPTER 5

DBT FOR EATING DISORDER

It is incredibly unpleasant and lonely to battle an eating issue. Therapy can be helpful if you are dealing with an eating disorder. Try some of these things in the meantime if you're struggling to recover from an eating disorder.

Write Your Story

Write your life's tale, paying special attention to the occasions that marked the beginning of your body consciousness. Go into great depth about what those occurrences meant and how they affected you. Make a timeline with major events marked, perhaps.

Change the Way You Think

Your thoughts shape your reality. Your thoughts can alter how your life plays out and how it unfolds. Examples of unfavorable thought patterns include: Having a black-or-white mindset in which obesity is caused by weight growth.

Highlighting the drawbacks. Letting only the negativity pass while removing the positives. Minor issues are viewed as catastrophes, and remarks are exaggerated.

Personalizing everything. You might think the world is against you or that people are passing judgment on you. They should have strict guidelines for how you and others should behave. This could cause you to hold yourself to arbitrary standards.

Changing Your Mind

Identify and stop the bad thoughts in your mind rather than letting them run automatically. Practice speaking and writing in a new, more encouraging manner to yourself.

Challenge your beliefs. Create new ones when you realize the old ones do not apply to your current situation. Have conversations with others about their beliefs. Rephrase and change those statements into positive ones. Even if you don't fully believe it, say aloud, "I am a fantastic person."

Above all, set aside some quiet time to clear your head and stop thinking constantly. You may hear the voice in your heart more clearly when your mind is calm.

Self-Acceptance Exercises

Spend the entire day (only one day) accepting who you are. When you exit the shower, if a voice criticizes your shortcomings, tell it to stop. You are experiencing a day of self-acceptance. Stop the thinking if you later find yourself using phrases like "dumb, awful, or ugly." Change it to "I am good, brilliant, and lovely." Recite positive statements aloud and in writing. Use the worksheet for self-acceptance.

Self-Acceptance Worksheet

Things I am good at:

1 _____
2 _____
3 _____

Compliments I have received:

1 _____
2 _____
3 _____

What I like about my appearance:

1 _____
2 _____
3 _____

Challenges I have overcome:

1 _____
2 _____
3 _____

I've helped others by:

1 _____
2 _____
3 _____

Things that make me unique:

1 _____
2 _____
3 _____

What I value the most:

1 _____
2 _____
3 _____

Times I've made others happy.

1 _____
2 _____
3 _____

Feel Your Feelings

Recall the tough emotional moments you went through before your eating disorder started.

Use your diary to give yourself chunks of no longer than fifteen minutes for each memory. Give a thorough account of what happened, and then after you're done, highlight with a different color pen the emotions you expressed.

Make a concerted effort to draw emotions from this experience.

Maybe illustrate them with drawings, or ask others who were present what they thought. Give your emotions the attention and validation that neither you nor anybody else has ever given them. Then consider how your eating disorder provided a way for you to manage these emotions. Give yourself the empathy and knowledge that you lacked back then.

Circle of Control

This is your circle of control. Write down thoughts and situations that make you lose your control over binge eating in each section.

Circle of Control

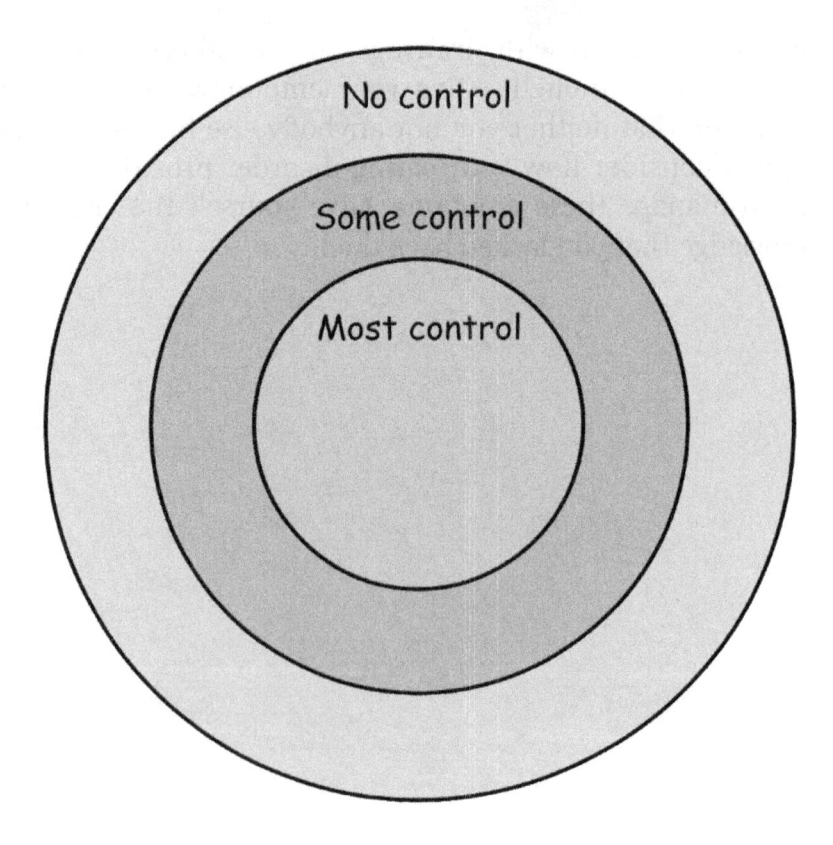

- No control
- Some control
- Most control

Depression and your Body

Depression is a symptom of binge eating. Identify your depression symptoms to control eating disorder.

Depression and My body

Color in the reactions that happen to your body when you feel sad or depressed.

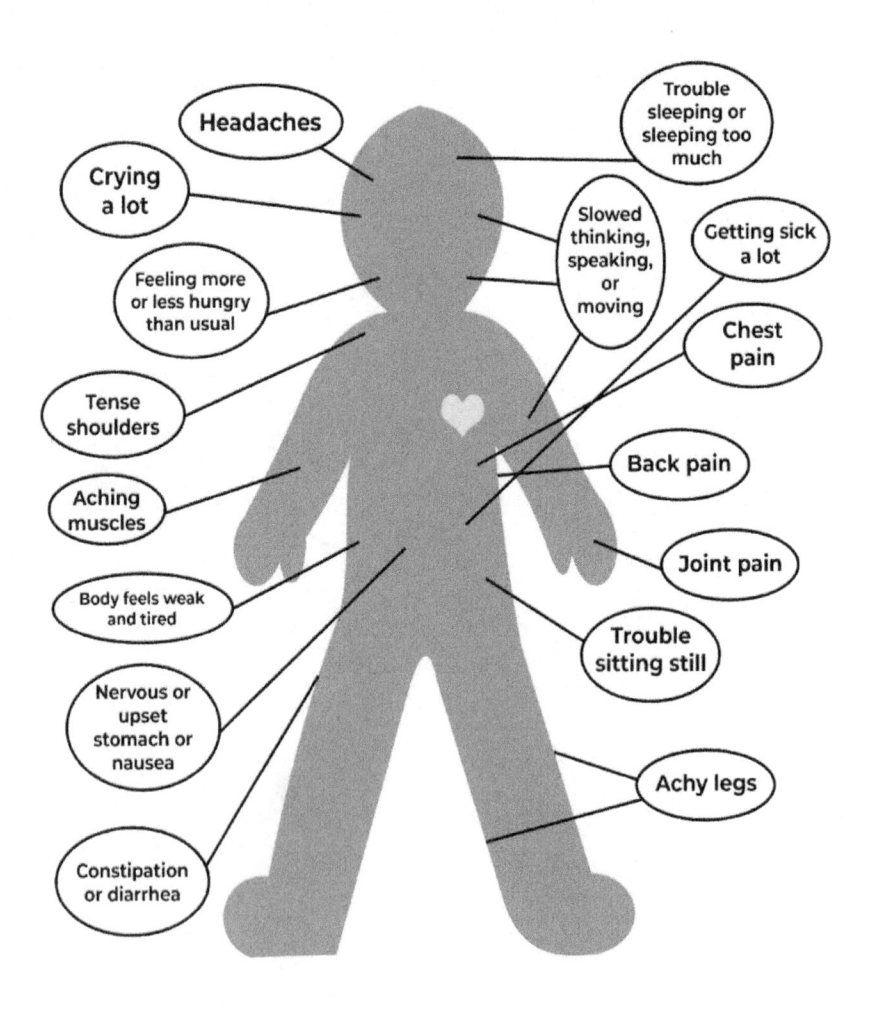

- Headaches
- Crying a lot
- Feeling more or less hungry than usual
- Tense shoulders
- Aching muscles
- Body feels weak and tired
- Nervous or upset stomach or nausea
- Constipation or diarrhea
- Trouble sleeping or sleeping too much
- Slowed thinking, speaking, or moving
- Getting sick a lot
- Chest pain
- Back pain
- Joint pain
- Trouble sitting still
- Achy legs

DBT Skills for Teens and Above

Set Goals

To overcome your eating disorder, use this sheet to set your daily goals.

Goal Setting Worksheet

Month_____

Goal_____

Why?

Steps to take

▪ _____

▪ _____

▪ _____

▪ _____

Deadline_____   ▪ Achieved

Potential Obstacles.....   How I'll Respond to Each

"Discipline is the bridge between goals and accomplishment." Jim Rohn

DBT Skills for Teens and Above

Use Affirmations

Affirmations

Write positive thoughts and affirmations you can say to yourself.

1	
2	
3	
4	
5	
6	
7	
8	
9	
10	

Be Gentle with Your Pain

You may have previously harmed yourself to cope with pain, which temporarily eased your suffering.

⁙ As an alternative, try to be kind to yourself.

Commit to accepting yourself where you are at this point in the process. When you are hurting deeply inside, resist the urge to numb yourself. Allow your emotions to run free while you are supported.

Here are some tips for coping with pain gently:

- Cry for some time and then stay strong.
- Cuddle up to a pet or teddy bear.
- Call a kind person who will treat you gently.
- Go on a walk. Be mindful of nature's beauty.
- Purchase or create a card of inspiration. Hang it or frame it.
- Play some music.
- Buy some fresh flowers for yourself.
- Create art, whatever you like.
- Create a poem to express your emotions.

⁙ Body Image Work

Dieting is ineffective. The majority of individuals who are unhappy with their bodies try diets, fail, and become self-conscious. Others succumb to an eating disorder, believing they have discovered the answer to the dieting conundrum.

Loving your body at whatever weight is one of the most challenging aspects of eating disorder treatment. Your set point is the weight range that your body prefers to maintain. Your genes determine your ideal weight, which is also healthy for you. Believe that you have a normal weight range and that your body will handle this very natural process. Everyone suffers from the pressure of being skinny.

Advice for enhancing self-image:

- Your body criticism should be addressed. Recite affirmations you have created for yourself, such as "My beauty is unique, and my body is a gift."
- Recognize each person's unique body and avoid comparing yourself to others. Models that are extremely lean or obese shouldn't be evaluated by their looks or you.
- Your body language should reflect this newfound pride as you walk and speak with dignity.
- Give your body praise for everything that it accomplishes for you. Treat it to massages, hot baths, scented candles, wholesome exercise, etc.
- Learn more about your body, respect your sexuality, and wear clothes that fit.
- With the knowledge that beauty on the outer reflects the beauty within, humbly accept praises.
- Stop scrutinizing particular physical parts so harshly in the mirror. Consider the big picture.
- Get rid of the weight scale.
- Consult self-help books on enhancing one's body image.
- Try using visualization and guided imagery.
- Practice yoga, dance, and other types of movement (as opposed to vigorous exercise).

✤ Relaxation is Key

Constant activity is a strategy to prevent issues or problems that need treatment and stress out the body. If it helps us avoid unpleasant feelings or memories, staying busy might turn into an addiction.

The most detrimental effect of excessive activity is that it causes you to lose touch with your inner self and deceives you into believing that your worth is only based on your achievements.

Then, rather than being a human "being," you are a human "doing." It can be challenging to unwind and relax. Try several relaxation techniques to calm your body and mind, and keep a diary nearby for ideas, adventures, and company.

Relaxation Methods: Practice Meditation

- Make opportunities for humor
- Take a stroll
- Take a shower
- Nap
- Peaceful candlelight dinner
- Watch your fish, stroke your cat, and lead the dog.
- Sit in a scenic or reverent location.
- Pray
- Tune in to calming music
- Practice deep breathing
- Practice Tai Chi or yoga
- Stretch
- Obtain a massage

CHAPTER 6

DBT FOR POST-TRAUMATIC STRESS DISORDER

Being present for or witnessing a terrifying or disturbing event can result in post-traumatic stress disorder, which can interfere with daily functioning and productivity. We go over a few DBT strategies in this chapter for managing its symptoms.

The disease known as post-traumatic stress disorder (PTSD) mostly affects veterans of the military, who are more likely than not to have witnessed a catastrophic occurrence on the battlefield. However, PTSD can naturally arise in reaction to a wide range of upsetting events, including sexual abuse, violent abuse, accidents, or any form of violence.

PTSD symptoms include recurrent flashbacks of the traumatic incident, increased anxiety, insomnia, moodiness, and avoidance of environments or social situations that can bring back memories.7.7 million persons in the United States have PTSD, even though women are more prone than males to experience this disorder.

PTSD symptoms can significantly negatively influence one's quality of life and can linger for years. Given this, it may be tempting to use unhealthy coping mechanisms to handle PTSD symptoms. Negative coping mechanisms can initially seem useful, but they can quickly become self-destructive. To dull your emotions, reduce tension, or quiet your thoughts, you can turn to recreational drugs or alcohol.

Alcohol and other drugs might initially make you feel better. Still, using them instead of behavioral therapy (DBT), which has been deemed a "safe and effective intervention" for this disease, could make you addicted.

What else can you do to keep your PTSD symptoms under control with DBT? Here are a few strategies you might wish to take into account.

De-Catastrophizing Worksheet

De-catastrophizing Worksheet

What are you worried about?

How likely is it that your worry will come true? Give examples of past experiences, or other evidence, to support your answer.

If your worry does come true, what's the worst that could happen?

If your worry does come true, what's most likely to happen?

If your worry comes true, what are the chances you'll be okay.....

In one week? _____%   In one month? _____%

Challenging Unhelpful Thoughts

Challenging Unhelpful Thoughts

A common negative thought I have is:

[ ]

Questions to ask myself:

Is this thought true?

[ ]

Do I have supporting evidence that this is true?

[ ]

What's the worst that could happen?

[ ]

What's the best that could happen?

[ ]

Am I having this thought because I'm unhappy about something else?

[ ]

Am I blaming someone else without taking responsibility?

[ ]

Am I jumping to conclusions?

[ ]

DBT Skills for Teens and Above

Trauma Triggers

My Trauma Triggers

Things that I see that trigger me.
_____

Smells that trigger me.
_____

Sounds that trigger me.
_____

I am triggered by following physical feelings in my body.
_____

Situations that trigger me.
_____

These places are triggers for me.
_____

Analyze your top 5 triggers with the following questions.
_____

Is this a trigger I can avoid or reduce? If so, how?
_____
_____

What coping skills can I use to manage my triggers when they can't be avoided?
_____
_____

Trauma Healing Worksheet

Healing Trauma Worksheet

Read the following questions, introspect your feelings and thoughts and provide the answers.

What is the situation that feels painful and brings traumatic memories? What happened that caused this situation? What happened then? What were your emotions?

| |
| |

Describe your actions, how others behave in the response?

| |
| |

How do other people behave in reaction in your actions?

_____

_____

DBT Skills for Teens and Above

Regain Focus Through Physical Activity

According to many people with PTSD diagnoses, finding a fun physical exercise that they can do daily has helped them manage their symptoms and lower stress levels. Following a childhood trauma diagnosis of PTSD, Rebecca Thorne discusses how jogging has helped her manage the negative symptoms affecting her life. She claims, "I am a runner and have [PTSD]." The connection between the two is only one of the many things I consider both while jogging and when I'm not.

Mindfulness Meditation

Meditation and insight meditation relaxation practices have effectively managed various diseases. A review of mindfulness-based PTSD therapy identifies a few interventions that have been proven successful in lowering avoidance and self-blame in those with the disease. Which are:

The purpose of mindfulness-based reducing stress (MBSR), a rigorous 8-week program centered on the practice of mindfulness meditation, is to teach participants how to direct their attention to their breathing and stop allowing distracting thoughts to take over.

Mindfulness-based exposure therapy, a 16-week non-trauma-focused program that incorporates mindfulness-based cognitive therapy MBCT techniques and favors safe and controlled publicity to avoid stimulation, focusing on self-compassion training, differs greatly from mindfulness-based cognitive therapy (MBCT), which is defined as "an adaptation of MBSR."

Mantrum repetition practice, which refers to "the silent repetition of a sacred word or phrase," appears to be effective in addressing anger, hyper arousal, or the condition of being always on guard, as well as symptoms of anxiety and depression.

Loving-kindness meditation was also found to be effective in increasing self-compassion and reducing symptoms of depression related to PTSD.

CHAPTER 7

IMPROVE SELF-ESTEEM THROUGH DBT

No matter what it takes, regardless of how successful we are, no matter how nice a parent, employee, or spouse we are—never enough. This is the great anguish of modern existence. There is always someone who causes us to feel inadequate in comparison, whether they are wealthier, leaner, sharper, or more powerful. Furthermore, failure in any form is unacceptable. Now what?

The self-esteem movement is one reaction that has taken place. Numerous books and magazine articles have been written over the years that advocate for self-esteem and explain how to build, maintain, and increase it. In our culture, the idea that having a high sense of self-worth is necessary for happiness and health has nearly become axiomatic. We are instructed to think well of ourselves constantly.

But it costs a lot to constantly think favorably about yourself. For instance, having a high sense of self-worth typically entails feeling exceptional and superior. Being characterized as average is offensive. (How was my performance last night? It was typical. Ouch!) Naturally, it is illogical for every person on the earth to be above normal at the same moment, which puts us in a difficult situation. To cope with this, we frequently attempt to exaggerate our accomplishments and minimize those of others.

Many societal issues, including racism, social inequity, and bullying, are rooted in the desire to boost one's self-esteem at the expense of others. Bullies typically have high self-esteem because picking on people who are weaker than they are is a simple method for them to feel more valuable. But you don't have to be a bully to improve your self-esteem. Here are some activities to help you.

My View of Me

Write down positive things that you think about yourself.

My View of Me

I was really happy when..._____

_____

Something that my friends like about me is..._____

_____

I'm proud of..._____

_____

My family was happy when I..._____

_____

Something that makes me unique is..._____

_____

DBT Skills for Teens and Above

Improve Self-Esteem Worksheet

Raise *Self Esteem* Now

I'm proud of these traits:

3 Factors which crush my self esteem

3 compliments which make me feel awesome

3 things I will do to handle the 3 factors above

People whose lives are more smooth-sailing or pleasant because of my presence

- ⬡
- ⬡
- ⬡
- ⬡
- ⬡

Notes

DBT Skills for Teens and Above

My Strengths

My Strengths Worksheet

In my eyes, my biggest strength is...

My friends and peers would say my biggest strength is...

My instructors would say my biggest strength is...

My family would say my biggest strength is...

Self-Confidence Worksheet

Self-Confidence Worksheet

You are amazing, really. Many things make you unique.
We can build our confidence by reminding ourselves of the things that make us great

List at least 5 compliments about yourself.

1 _____

2 _____

3 _____

4 _____

5 _____

Self-Esteem Journal

SELF-ESTEEM JOURNAL

Something good that happened to me today was_____

_____

_____

Something positive someone said about me_____

_____

A compliment that I would give myself today is_____

_____

Positive feelings that I experienced today!

_____   _____

_____   _____

I made someone else feel good when I_____

_____

I had a negative thought about myself when_____

_____

A different thought that I can have next time is_____

_____

Something I can do to make tomorrow a better day is_____

_____

Mindfulness Exercises for Improving Self-Esteem

It is necessary to be attentive, or be aware of the present-moment reality in a precise and balanced way for self-compassion. It entails being receptive to the truth of what is occurring and letting any thoughts, feelings, or sensations surface into awareness without opposition.

Why does mindfulness play such a crucial role in self-compassion?

To show compassion, you must first acknowledge that you are in pain. Though it can seem quite evident to you, pain isn't always obvious. Convince yourself that these thoughts of inadequacy are terrible and thus need a kind, compassionate response whenever you notice you are overweight or that your nose is too wide in the mirror? Is it your first reaction to console yourself when your supervisor summons you to the office and informs you that your work performance is subpar?

Most likely not. We certainly experience the anguish of falling short of our goals, but this sorrow is often overshadowed by the failure itself in our minds. Not to mention trying to calm and comfort ourselves while experiencing the emotional pain brought on by feelings of inadequacy, there isn't much brain room left over.

Humans have a built-in tendency to avoid pain, which is one reason we act this way. Our fight-or-flight reaction is triggered by pain, which indicates that something is wrong. It can be challenging to turn toward pain, hold it, and just be with it as it is because of our fundamental propensity to run from it.

By preventing us from avoiding unpleasant thoughts and feelings, mindfulness enables us to accept the reality of our experience—even when it's unpleasant. Being conscious also prevents us from "over identifying" with unfavorable ideas or feelings, allowing our adverse reactions to consume and sweep us away. This kind of contemplating inflates our opinions of our value.

But when we do it with awareness, we acknowledge our pain without making it seem worse. This enables us to take a more impartial attitude toward ourselves. Then, we can widen our hearts and allow our self-compassion to flourish.

Practice

Three Entrances

The three entrances into self-compassion are what makes it so beautiful. You have three options whenever you become aware of your misery.

1. You may be kind and understanding to yourself.
2. You might remind yourself that pain is a common aspect of being human.
3. Alternatively, you can be conscious of your thoughts and feelings to discover more equilibrium and calm.

It will be simpler to engage the other two self-compassion components after improving any of the three. Based on your attitude and the circumstances, you could find it easier to approach one doorway than another, but once you're inside, you're inside. No, whatever the circumstances of your life are at the time, you'll be in a condition of loving, connected presence (another way of characterizing the three elements of self-compassion). The power of self-compassion will have been shown to you, and it may change your life forever.

Practice

The Break from Self-Compassion

During the self-compassion break, you'll use a list of phrases you've learned to calm and comfort yourself when you're in pain.

1. Place both of your hands over your heart, pause, and enjoy comfort. You can also place your hands on any other area of your body, such as your tummy or your face, that you find relaxing and reassuring.
2. Inhale and exhale deeply.
3. Use the following phrases to comfort and reassure yourself (aloud or in your head):"This is a painful moment.Life is full of suffering.May I be compassionate to myself and show me the necessary compassion."

The first sentence, "This is a time of suffering," is meant to help you become aware of how uncomfortable you are. Other possible wordings for this expression include "This hurts," "I'm going through a pretty hard time right now," and so on.

The second phrase, "Suffering is part of life," is meant to serve as a gentle reminder that everyone experiences imperfection from time to time. Other alternative phrases are "This is part of being human," "Everyone feels this way sometimes," and so forth.

The third sentence, "May I be nice to myself at this moment?" is meant to help you experience the current moment with caring concern. Other suggested phrases include "May I accept myself as I am?" and "May I love and support myself right now?".

Your aim to be self-compassionate is clearly stated in the final sentence, "May I give myself the love I need?" You could also say things like "May I remember that I am deserving of compassion?" "May I show myself the same kindness I would show a good friend?" and similar things.

Choose the four phrases that feel the most natural to you and learn them by heart. Then, you may use these words as a technique to remind yourself to be kind to yourself the next time you criticize yourself or go through a trying moment. It's a useful technique to help relax and settle upsetting mental states.